BEHAVIORAL THEORY

DIALECTICAL STANCE AND STRATEGIES

Marcus Wright

Table of Contents

INTRODUCTION 3

CHAPTER ONE: BASICS OF DIALECTICAL BEHAVIORAL THERAPY 6

CHAPTER TWO: WHAT YOU NEED TO KNOW IN BEHAVIORAL THEORY 46

CHAPTER THREE: DIALECTICAL STANCE AND STRATEGIES 60

CHAPTER FOUR: PREPARING FOR THE INDIVIDUAL SESSION; WHAT YOU NEED TO KNOW 87

INTRODUCTION

DBT was initially designed to treat BPD, and has since been shown to be beneficial for all manner of other conditions. Fortunately, we now know it's quite effective for anyone with emotion-regulating issues, even if the cause is not linked to a psychiatric condition. DBT has become a widely sought-after therapy, because of its effectiveness in helping people learn to control their feelings more effectively. Unfortunately, too few practitioners are still sufficiently trained in DBT, given the number of people who are searching for this form of help with their issues. One of the motive of thus book is to provide clinicians with a basic understanding of the DBT philosophy, the techniques used in individual sessions that separate it from standard CBT, and the DBT skills themselves. The book is not meant as an effort to replicate Marsha Linehan's extraordinary work in any manner, shape, or type. In many respects her research was important in the world of psychotherapy.

Alternatively, my hope is to make DBT more available to clinicians who might be overwhelmed by it, thus making DBT more accessible to clients who would benefit from it. It is also extremely helpful for professionals in their own personal and professional lives to simply use the DBT techniques themselves. Not only will this help with your own learning, but it will also encourage you to say you are doing what you preach! It's hard to teach something to someone, if you don't do it yourself.

The book shows why, where, and how to apply the dialectical behavior therapy (DBT) concepts and techniques of interpersonal psychotherapy. While the first DBT book by Linehan (1993a) is a therapy textbook, this book is a reference guide, full of therapeutic vignettes and step-by-step explanations to help you see how you can use DBT with your clients.

For many clients with disabilities other than personality disorders, you can only use the DBT techniques and you may notice that some of these clients require only some of the skills; with example, certain clients do not need pain management or emotional communication skills because they are already well adjusted in these areas, but they still need skills to help them be more sensitive and handle t To clients with symptoms consistent with personality disorders, you can plan to integrate some of the uses of DBT learning theory in individual sessions, as well as demonstrate some or all of the skills. In the end, if you don't use DBT to treat BPD, the treatment is very flexible and can be used for any disorder

CHAPTER ONE: BASICS OF DIALECTICAL BEHAVIORAL THERAPY

WHAT IS DIALECTICAL BEHAVIOURAL THERAPY?

The type of cognitive behavioral therapy is dialectical behavioral therapy. Palmer refers to this as "a strange hybrid" of different treatments and strategies. Most people asked how the distinction between dialectical behavioral therapy and cognitive behavioral therapy is. Typically I reply that, in terms of skills, dialectical behavioral therapy is really just cognitive behavioral therapy using a different language, with the introduction of strategies of attentiveness and approval. Dialectical behavioral therapy removes the decision from cognitive behavioral therapy so that the thought of participants is not "false," "erroneous" or "distorted," with the goal of changing their attitude. Alternatively, dialectical behavioral therapy recognizes that there is an issue with how clients think, but the therapist then allows clients to consider that, rather than judging it, and then helps them to look at how they can make changes to make their thought more stable. Going at the entire model of Dialectical Behavioral Therapy instead of just the techniques, however, shows that this approach is quite distinct from cognitive behavioral therapy.

The main distinction is that Dialectical behavioral therapy is a treatment based on principles, whereas cognitive behavioral therapy appears to be a therapy based on guidelines (Swales & Heard, 2009). The psychiatrist implements specific procedures in Cognitive behavioral therapy; for example, when a person has panic attacks, a set of rules or techniques are practiced to handle fear, such as delivering psycho-education, practicing abdominal breathing, etc.

For DBT, however, the therapist is driven by values which allow the therapist to be more versatile. This is important when treating people who have trouble controlling their emotions—and particularly those with a BPD diagnosis—because these participants frequently have a variety of problems, making it hard to concentrate on just one thing in each session. When a person has a variety of problems, it is almost impossible to try to implement a highly structured treatment protocol that addresses just one of these problems (Swales & Heard, 2009) and would certainly be viewed by the client as invalidating. A second major difference between DBT and COGNITIVE BEAHVIOURAL THERAPY is in the provision of the medication. COGNITIVE BEAHVIOURAL THERAPY may be given either in a group or individual setting but rarely occurs concurrently in both, while DBT consists of four separate therapy modes: interpersonal counseling, community of techniques, and the therapy team and even telephone coversation(each of which will be illustrated later in this chapter). Unlike COGNITIVE BEAHVIOURAL THERAPY, DBT includes self-monitoring; but, using the Behavior Monitoring Sheets, it is brought to a different level of DBT.

DBT also differs from COGNITIVE BEAHVIOURAL THERAPY in the layout of individual sessions, presenting patterns and recovery steps within a continuum dictated by the nature and vulnerability of desired behaviours. DBT is also characterized by its use of a suicide risk and intervention protocol. Above and beyond therapy delivery; the use of the therapeutic relationship of DBT is founded on coping philosophy and quite different from the methodology of COGNITIVE BEAHVIOURAL THERAPY. Since DBT is a behaviorally oriented treatment, the practitioner views BPD as a form of learned behaviour. The DBT approach emphasizes the importance of understanding the causes for unhealthy habits and the contingencies that sustain certain patterns and help clients unlearn these harmful behaviors. The DBT therapist makes every effort to promote this by establishing a strong and sincere relational relationship with the client, which can then be used in a variety of ways to help clients make the necessary changes. Participants learn multiple strategies in COGNITIVE BEAHVIOURAL THERAPY to help improve distorted thinking; in DBT, participants are orientated to accept themselves as they are, and then to learn tools to help them alter habits that are dysfunctional or troublesome in some way. The counseling partnership (including self-disclosure by the psychiatrist) becomes another method used by the therapist to help clients make the important improvements.

Having a relationship with a safe, positive figure is particularly important for clients who have trouble controlling their feelings, as you will soon see when we look at BPD's principle of bio socials. Nevertheless, before we discuss the hypothesis of how emotional dysregulation occurs, we must first describe dysregulation of the emotion itself.

WHAT IS EMOTION DYSREGULATION

According to Linehan (1993a), a mixture of high emotional intensity or weakness and an inability to control or modulate one's emotions results in emotional dysregulation.

EMOTIONAL VULNERABILITY

A biological predisposition leads to emotional vulnerability or personality in which a person is born more sensitive to emotion than most. Such individuals tend to personally react to things other people wouldn't normally react to. Their emotional reaction is usually more extreme than the situation warrants, and it takes them longer to recover from that reaction than the average person, and to return to their emotional center. The concept of emotional vulnerability is close to that of the highly sensitive person that Elaine Aron (1996) wrote extensively about. Aron claims that possessing a reactive nervous system is a relatively common neurological function, believing that this high level of sensitivity is felt by around 15 to 20 per cent of the population. Aron postulates that people who are highly sensitive are more quickly aroused (reacting emotionally to things other people wouldn't normally respond to) and over-aroused (experiencing a more intense reaction than the situation warrants). Blakeslee and Blakeslee (2007) support the idea that there is a psychological, neurological foundation to this elevated emotional awareness.

In addition, Koerner and Dimeff (2007) note that variations in the central nervous system have been shown to play a role in making a person more emotionally unstable, and that these changes in the central nervous system could be related to a variety of factors, including biology or stress during fetal development or early life.

Inability to regulate emotions

Emotion control applies to the mechanisms we use to reduce, maintain or increase an emotion or parts of an emotion (Werner & Gross, 2010) (unconsciously, intentionally or perhaps with a considerable amount of effort). In most cases, we want to reduce the intensity of the painful emotions or, if possible, make them go away entirely. But sometimes we simply want to increase an emotion (for example, someone who feels sad might want to increase pleasure feelings). Both of these are seen as controlling feelings.

It's important to note that controlling feelings doesn't involve hiding emotions or trying to hide them from others; in those situations, the emotions are still there and uncontrolled, though they may be concealed. The aim of emotion regulation is instead to maintain a controlled state of conscious manipulation of the emotional experience and speech (Greenberg & Paivio, 1997). It is generally difficult for people who are unable to control their feelings to recognize or mark the emotion they feel, to explain why they feel that way, and to convey the emotion effectively. Due to this result,, they are unable to handle the feelings they feel. Unlike the aspect of emotional vulnerability to this equation, the ability to regulate one's emotions seems to be affected more by the atmosphere in which an individual grows up. For starters, Miller, Rathus, and Linehan (2007) point to research suggesting early traumatic encounters have a significant impact on the ability of individuals to control their emotions. On the positive side this suggests that children develop better ability to control their feelings as their parents react in an appropriate and compassionate way to their display of painful emotions (Thompson & Goodman, 2010).

Koole (2009) also states that the capacity of children to control their feelings is greatly influenced by the nature of their social interactions with caregivers. Koole also states that the ability of people to control changes in feelings throughout the course of life continues to improve with age. And, the good news is that if they didn't learn them as children, we should give them the tools they need to control their emotions.

THE BIOSOCIAL THEORY OF BORDERLINE PERSONALITY DISORDER

Since Linehan originally developed her biosocial hypothesis to aid in identifying and managing borderline personality disorder (1993a), in this article I'll apply only to BPD. At the conclusion of this segment, though, I will take a look by two explanations of how researchers continue extending this hypothesis to other diseases. According to the biosocial theory of Linehan (1993a), emotional dysregulation (emotional weakness plus the failure to control one's emotions) derives from a biological predisposition and the relationship of the person with the environment (Miller et al., 2007). We have just looked at the biological predisposition — the aspect of emotional dysregulation— and there is an array of research showing that some people are born just more responsive than others. This does not not mean that all born emotionally sensitive people will develop BPD or other mental health problems. That is just one part of the equation; the other part is the world in which a child grows up. Problems tend to arise when a person who is biologically fragile faces a pervasively invalidating climate (Linehan, 1993a).

The Invalidating Environment

Miller and colleagues (2007) describe an invalidating atmosphere as one in which there is a propensity to reject or react unpredictably and improperly to the private experiences of the child, and in particular to private experiences such as impulses, physical sensations, and thoughts that are not supported by evidence to prove that this is the experience of the child in reality. In other terms, when a child shows a feeling (a private experience), the adults in her world criticize her for this experience (e.g. advising her that she shouldn't feel that way or that she's overreacting); telling her that her experience is false or diminishing her experience; shaming her for complaining about her experience; dismissing her interpretation of the event; etc. In invalidating situations, the assumption is typically that the child should be able to control the manifestation of his / her impulses (which is impractical due to the child's emotional vulnerability) and should not show "negative" feelings (Miller et al., 2007). When she can not fulfill these standards, the community punishes her for sharing such negative experiences and only reacts to her emotional presentations if she escalates, effectively forcing her to switch in extreme ways between stifling her feelings and expressing emotions to get support (Koerner & Dimeff, 2007).

The other important piece about invalidating situations is that the idea is often communicated that the person should be able to solve the problem they are dealing quite easily. Nevertheless, in this type of environment, the emotionally sensitive infant is never properly taught skills such as emotion regulation and problem solving. So the idea is she should be able to help herself feel better, but she's never learned the skills to do so. It obviously puts her in for disappointment and leads to self-invalidation (for example, convincing herself that everyone thinks she should be able to do this, and punishing herself because she can't). There are many ways an atmosphere can become invalidating. Several instances are mentioned on the next four pages.

THE POOR FIT

Kids are sometimes born into families they just don't fit properly into. An example would be an artistic girl born into a family where her parents and siblings are sensible who hard-working, and see her imagination as a waste of time— something that will never give her enough money to be successful and therefore not to be sought. These parents may have the best interests of their child at heart; they want her to be successful and happy but they stop her from following her talent because they don't believe it's in her best interests. In this invalidating climate, the emotionally vulnerable child will grow up thinking like her ability to be artistic is false and therefore something is wrong with her for wanting to pursue it. She will also feel isolated and unlike the rest of her family.

THE CHAOTIC HOME

Many people have additional challenges that make providing a validating climate impossible for them. Maybe the parents themselves were invalidated as infants, so they never knew how to provide affirmation for themselves or others. Families who have their own mental health problem or an illness, or who are financially unstable and therefore have a hard time getting the necessities of life, will find it much more difficult to provide their children with an emotionally safe and healthy atmosphere. It's also important to note that children who are highly sensitive to emotion can be the source of at least some of the home confusion.

Miller and colleagues (2007) suggest that having a child in the family that is emotionally vulnerable can be so overwhelming that the family system gets overwhelmed, possibly leading to a debilitating setting. In other meaning, when an emotionally vulnerable child is born into a family where others do not possess this characteristic, it is impossible for the rest of the family to understand and this in itself can cause disabilities because parents are upset with the child and do not know how to help. We've all heard a parent reminding an upset kid, "Don't be stupid; there's nothing to be scared of," advising a wounded child, "Stop crying," or saying to an angry child, "You're not very good." Those parents don't mean invalidating the infant; they're just feeling frustrated and they don't know how to help their child efficiently in that moment. And, for an emotionally vulnerable girl, these signals over time add up to the idea that she is doing something wrong.

THE ABUSIVE HOME

In BPD to evolve, violence does not have to exist, but it is certainly not uncommon. For evidence, one study (Stone, 1981) showed that 75 percent of the twelve hospitalized patients with a BPD diagnosis had an incest history. A study of the map (Herman, 1986) showed that 67 percent of twelve BPD psychiatric outpatients had a history of childhood or juvenile violence. And a retrospective analysis (Bryer, Nelson, Miller, & Krol, 1987) found that 86 per cent of 14 psychiatric BPD patients had experienced sexual harassment before the age of 16. For example a hostile workplace is the most is considered the highest environment that is invalidate. It can take many forms, from physical abuse in reaction to the child's display of negative emotions or for the child's "own benefit" to sexual abuse in which the abuser assures the child it's okay but instructs her not to say anybody, potentially punishing her or those she loves if she reveals. To relation to this victim invalidation, several victims are further invalidated because they tell someone about the violence and are disbelieved, accused of lying and perhaps even blamed for the abuse (Linehan, 1993a). While being a passive form of abuse, negligence can be just as harmful.

Through abuse, the child learns that whatever she does, her desires, wishes, and feelings will be completely disregarded (invalidated)—unless, of course, she escalates her actions to the point that her caregivers cannot tolerate them any longer.

OTHER INVALIDATING ENVIRONMENTS

Although we generally look to the family and home setting to see where the problems lie, invalidation can also arise outside the household: at school, at work, at the babysitter's house, although spending time with other family members while participating in extracurricular activities such as athletics or clubs, and so on. Kids stay a lot of time at school, of course, and if the classroom belongs to an unhealthy environment.kid who is emotionally vulnerable. Types of out - of-home invalidation include a child with caring issues (such as ADD) whose teacher accuses her of not trying or being deliberately disruptive in class, a child who is abused by classmates (such as being mocked for crying), a child who has trouble making friends, or a child whose coach insists on the bad and advises her she should be expected to do more or do better.

A TRANSACTIONAL MODEL

It is important to emphasize that the biosocial hypothesis is dialectical or transactional, implying that experiences between the world and the person take place over time, slowly contributing to their attachment to each other and the creation of BPD. Therapists are therefore advised to interpret consumer attitudes as natural reactions in response to environmental stimuli (Lynch, Trost, Salsman, & Linehan, 2007). It is not possible to blame the individual for being "too easy," and the atmosphere is not entirely at fault. The disease would have been unlikely to develop without the relationship between these two factors.

Applying the Biosocial Theory to Other Disorders

It is highly sensible to apply the biosocial hypothesis to the creation of other disorders, because emotional dysregulation is a component of so many different diseases, and this issue may contribute to emotional isolation through participating in unhealthy behaviors such as drug use, disordered feeding, self-harm, and so on. I'm sure anyone who deals with people with mental health issues regularly sees the effect an invalidating climate can have on individuals. While the biosocial hypothesis has been published so far only for BPD, other personality disorders, and eating disorders, it would also refer to many people with other illnesses in my professional experience, and potentially to persons who may not have a diagnosable mental illness but have trouble controlling their emotions. Right now let's take a quick look at the biosocial hypothesis theories about other personality disorders and eating disorders.

Other personality disorders.

Lynch and Cheavens (2007) suggested the idea of adapting the biosocial paradigm to personality disorders other than BPD. They propose that a biological predisposition to an increased negative effect interacts with an invalidating atmosphere that promotes unhealthy modes of avoidance in a transactional manner to create the cognitive, emotional, and behavioral behaviors typically seen in personality disorders, especially in the form of difficulties in sustaining interpersonal relationships, emotional regulation, and contents.

Eating disorders.

Several scholars have looked at adapting the biosocial hypothesis to binge-eating disorder and bulimia, based on the idea that individuals indulge in disordered eating behaviors because of an inability to regulate their impulses (Wisniewski, Safer, & Chen, 2007). In the same way, Safer, Telch, and Chen (2009) argue and inadequate mechanism for controlling feelings, making certain people unable to properly control, evaluate, embrace, and alter their emotional experience. Safer and colleagues theorize that these challenges arise from getting the message given to the emotionally vulnerable child that she should be able to regulate her feelings and solve problems even though she has not been shown the skills to do so.

THE DIALECTICAL THEORY OF DBT

Linehan (1993a) was greatly influenced by the philosophy of dialectics in developing her paradigm of therapy, a dynamic philosophical and scientific concept with three main principles: • Everything is intertwined or interrelated. This theory allows us to comprehend the value of a system-wide approach to the recognition and implementation of transition. It also tells us that the client's actions and reactions will affect the psychiatrist, who in turn will effect the client, and so on (Feigenbaum, 2007).

• Truth is not stagnant but in a constant process of change (Swales & Heard, 2009).

• Reality (which is always evolving) can be sought through the combination or convergence of different (and likely opposite) opinions (Feigenbaum 2007). Clearly this notion goes contradictory to the typical black-and-white thinking of people with emotional dysregulation.

So what does that mean for treatment, exactly? Miller and colleagues (2007) state that thought dialectically means looking at both viewpoints in a situation, and then moving at synthesizing certain views that might be opposed. In other words, clients (and therapists!) must learn to tolerate the fact that two things that seem to be the contrary will coexist. Therapist and counselor must note, in thought dialectically, that reality is not stagnant and set, But is changing constantly and full of apparent contradictions; for example, the assumption that clients are doing their best they can and that, at the same time, they must work harder and do more. Another common example, particularly for a person with emotion-regulating problems, is the possibility of feeling two apparently opposing feelings at the same time; here is the role of the therapist to help the client understand that, for example, she may love her husband and at the same time be really angry about him.

Dialectic reasoning means we have to cultivate tolerance while also continuing to work for improvement. Through DBT, this is the main dialectic— both practitioner and counselor need to embrace the person as they are and also need to continue to work on improving negative or self-destructive habits. But there are many other forms in which dialectical reasoning comes into play in therapy. For starters, as conflicts occur in therapy or in the life of the client, dialectical thought makes both therapist and client learn to look for what is missing out of their experience, so they can seek to see the different perspectives picture or (Basseches, 1984).

Lynch and colleagues (2007) emphasize that one of the most significant prevalent dialectical contradictions is the belief that an inappropriate or self-destructive action, such as cutting, can be both therapeutic (helping people to reduce their short-term emotional distress) and pathological (because self-injury results in a number of negative effects). In this question, client and therapist need to consider the balance of these two obvious opposites; for example, validating the client's need for some help while at the same time aiding the client in acquiring and using strategies that will not worsen the anxiety (Lynch et al., 2007). Dialectic philosophy means recognizing that all views can have elements that are both true and wrong. In counseling, understanding that polarizations are imminent is important; having a dialectical viewpoint means recognizing this inevitability, waiting for the polarizations and not encouraging the elf to get caught up in them when they arise. Lynch and colleagues (2007) note that the fundamental characteristic of Zen is this dialectical idea of taking the middle path, and that DBT uses these ideas to help clients behave more successfully and lead more healthy lives.

THE DIALECTICAL BEHAVIOURAL THERAPY MODEL

The Design DBT consists of four elements. While my professional experience has been that DBT can be provided successfully to individuals without all of these aspects being included, the bulk of DBT literature for BPD focuses at the entire model, which includes skills training program, individual therapy, telephone meeting, and consulting team.

Skills Training Group

The skills training program is a formal psychoeducation community model intended to improve and strengthen client capability. The program is broken into four groups once a week: core communication skills, behavioral productivity skills, emotion regulation skills, and coping skills for anxiety.

Key perception skills: Linehan (1993b) splits awareness down into smaller parts to make it easy for clients to grasp and integrate it into their lives. Attention in addressing BPD is aimed at reducing self-confusion, but attentiveness is also effective in many other respects.

Increasing self-awareness allows clients become more conscious of their feelings, desires, and impulses and slowly learn how to manage them properly. Through carefulness, clients also learn to tolerate the thoughts, emotions, and urges that they can't do anything about it, come to see that internal experiences don't have to be acted upon, but can simply be acknowledged, and these experiences gradually dissipated.

Emotional communication skills: These techniques are aimed at helping clients reduce the emotional uncertainty that often arises in their life and are primarily concerned with how could we be more assertive. Clients are taught how to ponded want to get out of an experience (for example, if they have a specific goal, if they want to preserve or even strengthen their friendship, or When they wish to keep or boost their self-respect) and then they are taught skills that will increase their chances of achieving this goal.

Skills controlling emotions: The purpose of this module is to reduce mood liability. Clients are taught general emotional knowledgeFor eg, why we need it and why we don't want to get rid of it even though they can sometimes be very traumatic. Clients think about the link between their emotions, perceptions, and actions, and they can have an effect on others by modifying one of these. This program stresses self-validation along with other skills to help clients control their feelings more effectively.

Distress management skills: These skills are also known as disaster survival skills and the aim is simply to help people navigate emergencies without making things worse by engaging in problematic behaviors such as suicide attempts, self-harm, substance abuse, and so on. Such skills help clients soothe and escape from the problem, rather than focus on it and eventually act on the impulses that surround the painful emotions. Teaching lessons in group format as opposed to in individual therapy is done for a variety of reasons: First, clients with anger management problems sometimes switch from one problem to another, and it is incredibly difficult to teach techniques in an individual session when the client naturally wants help with the current crisis. Furthermore, feedback is an important aspect of any group setting, as each person has the benefit of being in a group with others that have similar problems. The advantage to classes is that as each participant benefits from the perspectives of fellow group members, the learning experience can be much richer. Ultimately, since relationship problems frequently occur in classes, this can be a great environment for learning the teaching skills and also helps participants to seek community therapy instruction on how to use the skills to act more effectively.

Individual Therapy

Clients usually undergo single appointments once a week with a DBT practitioner. Individual interventions aim to help participants use group-learned skills to minimize target habits such as suicidality, self-harm, drug use, and so forth. As with group sessions, the structure and style of individual sessions is very simple.

Telephone Consultation

Telephone coaching is used for the use of expertise to mentor clients. Telephone counseling is intended to be a short experience to help clients determine which skills might be most helpful in the situation they face, and to help them overcome barriers to the successful use of these capabilities and to respond.

Consultation Team

Linehan says "Without the band, there is no DBT" (2011). The DBT therapy team's composition can vary depending on the circumstances of the psychiatrist. The staff is usually composed of all the clinicians in a DBT clinic: social workers, counselors, physicians, and anyone else involved for DBT members in individual therapy and skills training programs. This is fairly straightforward for the clinicians working in outpatient environments. But it gets a little more complex for those of us who work in private practice. Because the team is important to keep the therapists on course of their work, private therapists may want to build a team of other private DBT therapists in their field, or even online, as long as confidentiality is maintained.

Whatever it consists of in the situation, the unit is used in two ways: first, to provide guidance to professionals and to help them continue to develop their skills by using the DBT approach to work with clients; and second, to resolve situations. The team helps the client ensure she adheres to DBT methods and procedures during case review. The squad also tackles the burnout and ineffectiveness emotions. The team uses DBT strategies such as taking a dialectical approach and being non-judgmental in group sessions to keep team members from getting caught up in power struggles and other conflicts which can hinder the team and the therapy process.

BEING FLEXIBLE WITH DBT

My assumption is that a bit of DBT is safer than none sometimes. Of example, for many clients, I find the DBT skills invaluable, particularly the mindfulness and acceptance skills that many clients have never mastered in other treatment modalities. It's also invaluable to affirm people and encourage them to trust themselves, given the environment in which they grew up. Furthermore, integrating the biosocial paradigm into your work, while eliminating the tendency to blame people for their actions, will have significant benefits for both your clients and the counseling relationship, which will help to reduce the risk of burning you out.

RESEARCH ON DIALECTICAL BEHAVIOURAL THERAPY FOR Border line

Personality disorder AND OTHER DISORDERS

After DBT came into being in 1980, much research has concentrated on its efficacy as a cure for BPD and, more specifically, for other diseases. In this section, I will review the BPD DBT studies as well as model modifications, and then look at the new literature on using DBT to tackle other mental health issues.

DIALECTICAL BEHAVIORAL THERAPY for Borderline Personality Disorder

The first psychotherapeutic therapy for BPD studied in a clinical trial was DBT. The original DBT trial was compared with a year to therapy as normal and concluded that DBT was a better medication, particularly in terms of decreases in levels of self-harm, over dosage and hospitalization (Linehan, Armstrong, Suarez, Allmon, & Heard, 1991). Similar findings were found in other trials conducted since the original trial (e.g., Koons et al. 2001; Verheul et al. 2003). Additionally, in 2006, Linehan and collaborators conducted another review, this time compared DBT for BPD to therapy offered by community practitioners— community therapists who were chosen because of their expertise in that they described as non-behavioral, or mostly psychodynamic. The results of this study have confirmed that DBT is a superior therapy, with decreases in suicide attempts and levels of hospitalization (Linehan et al., 2006).

Adapting DBT

Several scholars updated the initial DBT model in an effort to minimize the length of the original twelve-month recovery plan used by Linehan to reduce costs. Of example, of patients with BPD on an inpatient unit, Bohus and colleagues (2004) modified the model to provide a faster, three month version of DBT. Additionally, Kleindienst and colleagues (2008) considered three months of DBT to be highly effective in supporting BPD clients on an inpatient unit, and the results were sustained in a two-year follow-up. Moreover, an outpatient study suggested a modified six-month version of DBT was effective in treating BPD (Stanley, Brodsky, Nelson, & Dulit, 2007). Clearly there is a need for further work to assess the feasibility of modified DBT models. Yet my professional experience was that you don't have to provide the clients with the "real" or full DBT model to benefit — especially clients without BPD. In fact, given that services are often limited these days, I believe we need to be more pragmatic so that patients can still provide some kind of DBT therapy, even if the full model cannot be adhered to.

DBT for Other Psychiatric Disorders

More and more work on the use of DBT to treat diseases other than BPD is under way. I'll only provide a brief summary here because of the vast body of research. Harned and colleagues noted in a 2008 study that several studies have found DBT to be effective in reducing the behaviors associated with Axis I conditions, including alcohol use, bulimia, binge-eating disorder, insomnia, and anxiety. In the following cases too, DBT was studied:

• Harley, Sprich, Safren, Jacobo, and Fauva (2008) discovered improvements thate are great in treatment-resistant depression patients.

• Preliminary research showed DBT to be effective in the diagnosis of juvenile bipolar disorder (Goldstein, Axelson, Birmhaer, & Brent, 2007) and DBT techniques to be useful in the management of adult bipolar disorder (Van Dijk, Jeffery, & Katz, in press).

- The teaching of DBT strategies was described as possible and effective in changing the actions of teenagers with oppositional defiant disorder (Nelson-Gray et al. 2006).

- DBT-enhanced habit-reversal therapy has been shown to be a promising solution to trichotillomania, with six-month follow-up changes (Keuthen et al., 2011).

- A promising method has been shown to be DBT adapted to intensively treat post-traumatic stress disorder (PTSD) due to childhood sexual abuse (Steil, Dyer, Priebe, Kleindienst, & Bohus, 2011).

- Perepletchikova and colleagues (2011) have tailored DBT to treat children with nonsuicidal self-harming behaviours; the findings have been positive, with a significant increase in functional coping skills and a great decrease in depression and the thoughts of suicidal.

Rajalin, Wickholm-Pethrus, Hursti, and Jokinen (2009) used DBT-based skills training for suicide attempted family members. Results indicated significant reductions in the stress on patients, better emotional health and greater satisfaction with the patient relationship.

Ironically, DBT is also used by physicians to treat diseases and problems not linked to Axis I conditions. For example, ever shed and colleagues (2003) used DBT to alleviate rage in male forensic patients, and found that the DBT group made greater gains relative to patients receiving care as normal. More recently, Sakdalan, Shaw, and Collier (2010) reported that DBT decreased risk levels in suicidal forensic patients with intellectual disabilities, and Drossel, Fisher, and Mercer (2011) found that DBT helped loved one's caregivers with dementia increase their effective therapeutic support, enhance their psychosocial tolerance, increase their ability to cope, improve their mental well-being, Also, some scholars have been working on modified versions of DBT therapy for conditions other than BPD in the hope of reducing the duration and resulting treatment costs. Lynch, Trost, Salsman, and Linehan (2007) mention two studies suggesting that teaching in DBT techniques followed by only limited individual therapy may be effective for less serious psychological diseases. That is not exhaustive, despite the length of this "brief" survey. Numerous other studies have explored the efficacy of DBT in the diagnosis of BPD and other diseases. Ideally, however, this brief analysis has highlighted DBT's versatility and adaptability.

CHAPTER TWO: WHAT YOU NEED TO KNOW IN BEHAVIORAL THEORY
REINFORCEMENT

Reinforcing a behavior makes the behavior somehow more likely to happen again. There are various ways of doing this: primarily through positive strengthening, negative reinforcement, and intermittent reinforcement.

POSITIVE REINFORCEMENT

Through positive reinforcement, when participating in a certain action something that the person sees as good occurs. Although bonuses are an apparent and straightforward form of positive reinforcement, the process may be much subtler and more nuanced. For example, say a client recently asked you to see him more often for therapy sessions and you declined the offer, saying you only attend to clients once a week. The client then attempts suicide and is hospitalized for two weeks, then he calls you while in the hospital and asks you to see him for the time being twice a week to get him through this situation. If you agree, you provide positive reinforcement for his attempted suicide by giving him something he wants as a result of suicidal conduct.

NEGATIVE REINFORCEMENT

Don't be fooled by the term negative reinforcement. This is not a matter of deterrence. It is still enhancement, but in this case it happens by eliminating something that the person finds aversive. In other words, promoting a behaviour adversely means that something that the person finds uncomfortable will be omitted after a certain behavior happens, making it more likely that in the future the individual will participate in that same behavior in order to have the unpleasant experience eliminated again. Imagine a customer who becomes depressed and shamed over his slashing behaviour. When you're trying to analyze why he cut himself last week, he starts yelling at you and threatens to leave. When you concede and agree to change the subject, you have only validated the client adversely by eliminating the aversive experience of having to discuss his self-harming actions.

INTERMITTENT REINFORCEMENT

The positive or negative reinforcement occurs only occasionally in intermittent reinforcement, rather than every time the behavior takes place. In fact, this is one of the most successful ways to reinforce a behavior, as the person never knows when it will be strengthened. For gambling the most important example is. The slot machine intermittently reinforces the person to place coins in the slot and pull the handle, and a winning hand is dealt every now and then to the card player. Remember the customer whose wife broke up with him recently. He calls her on a daily basis, having difficulty accepting this. She doesn't answer his calls most often, but every now and then she gives in and speaks to him; even if only to confirm that the relationship is over. This intermittent reinforcement of responding to his calls from time to time keeps him calling her regularly in the hopes she will respond again.

SOME POINTERS ON REINFORCEMENT

In terms of strengthening, there are a few important points to consider. First, everybody has different reinforcers. What is aversive or rewarding to one person may have different functions for the next person. For example, while one client may enjoy talking about his self-harm outside of sessions because he knows that triggers emotions in others such as surprise, interest, or even disgust, another client may be ashamed and go to extreme lengths to conceal any signs of self-harm. Therefore, learning what is aversive and what reinforces particular clients is important.

 The second point to remember is that just because you know that you may perpetuate a behaviour you don't want, that doesn't mean you shouldn't act the way you want to. It just gives you more detail to remember, and may allow you to set firm boundaries before you act.

For example, in the case of the client who attempted suicide after being refused additional appointments, you may accept that after all, the client needs some extra support and you may want to be pragmatic about your one-week cap for a short period of time. It's perfectly fine for you to do this, but you might want to tell the client explicitly that you've changed your mind not because of the attempted suicide, but because you didn't realize how much distress he was in. You may also want to set new boundaries, such as being transparent about how long you're able to see him more often and whether there will be any kind of repercussions (e.g. going to one-weekly meetings) if another suicide attempt happens.

CONSEQUENCES

The term consequence refers to the effect, outcome or result of something that happened earlier. When we look at the consequences of a person's behaviour, we ask what happened after the person took action. There are two primary types of consequences: negative and positive.

NEGATIVE CONSEQUENCES

Most often, we speak about consequences in terms of negative outcomes: a person drops his medications and then starts to suffer mood disturbance and suicidal thoughts and engages in reckless behaviour, such as drinking and driving.

POSITIVE CONSEQUENCES

When you keep in mind that an effect is merely the outcome or product of something that happened earlier, it's easier to understand that the outcomes don't have to be negative, even though it's common to think of them this way. We can be constructive too. The woman who attempted suicide got the care and support she didn't have access to on a limited income as a single mother. While clinicians are usually very good at helping clients see the negative effects of their actions, there is a tendency to forget that there are also positive effects that serve to sustain the nature of the problem.

Of example, practical action also has implications and if clients notice that, it's beneficial to receive positive reinforcement to behave in healthy ways. An example would be a person who tells his mother that his feelings feel out of control and, as a result, he gets positive emotional support from his mother.

Shaping

You can shape an individual's behavior by reinforcing behaviors that are close to the desired behavior. For starters, Jeremy, a young man aged 18, was on probation for attacking his ex-friend. He was living with his parents back home and dealing with rage, often punching holes in the walls and screaming and swearing at his father. If he were to continue living with his parents, he would have to channel his vengeance elsewhere.

Jeremy said he would leave the situation as soon as he began to feel upset and go to his bedroom in the cellar, where he could scream and yell. (His parents knew about this intention and decided not to bother him.) He set up a punching bag in the basement so that he could get his frustration out on it, and there was a concrete wall in the cellar where he could smash pillows and other unbreakable items to help ease his rage. I provided reinforcement in the form of positive feedback when Jeremy reported that he was not taking his anger out on his parents any more. So we set up a system where Jeremy would praise himself if he went one day without taking out his frustration on his friends, and gradually expanded the time frame to a week. I helped shape the actions of Jeremy in this manner, so that it was similar to what we needed. From there, I helped Jeremy and his need for these new avenues to express his frustration and discover ways to express the emotion more healthily.

Modeling

Modeling essentially demonstrates somebody else's behavior to imitate. In DBT, modeling the use of techniques in therapy is essential for clinicians. For starters, when you're sitting with a frustrated, loud-speaking, and gesticulating customer, you're demonstrating by speaking softly and being still and quiet. It's normal for therapists to feel feelings in therapy, of course, but if you get upset and respond to the customer by shouting back or telling him to leave, you don't set a good example. If we don't use them ourselves, how can we expect our clients to practice on these complicated skills?

One excellent opportunity arises to model skills when the therapeutic relationship needs to be repaired. Linehan (1993a), as you may remember from the introduction, states that therapists are fallible. If you have messed up, please excuse yourself to the client. If you made a mistake, confess it. Recognize that your feelings are hurt or you were upset when the client blamed you for something or that he failed to complete his homework for the third week in a row. Note that you are also alive, so this is a human relationship. Having that in mind and behaving as if you're human (although a skillful one!) will help you form the actions you want the customer to know.

Clients also learn actions by watching other individuals, of course, and unfortunately that means they will not always imitate healthy behaviour. If this is the case, it can improve when clients know where they have learned this behaviour so they can choose to stick with the behavior or learn a new way of behaving.

Contingency Management

Contingency refers to a situation between two phenomena in which, if one happens, the other is more likely to occur. For example, if a psychiatrist has known from past experiences that if he cancels a client's visit, the client is likely to experience emotional distress and participate in some sort of self-destructive behavior, that is a possibility.

In DBT, contingency strategies are based on the assumption that the results of a behaviour will influence the risk of the patient deciding to participate in that activity again. Accordingly, risk management is about using psychological contingencies to support the individual. In other words, therapists need to be aware of how their behavior is likely to affect specific clients so that they do not inadvertently strengthen unwanted behaviors or punish or neglect to reinforce desired behaviours. So if the aforementioned therapist knows that his client is likely to act in a self-destructive manner because he has to cancel his appointment, he can try to manage this contingency by setting a limit that if the client is self-harming, he will not take additional telephone calls from the client for a certain period of time (as this would provide positive reinforcement for self-harming behaviour). When further phone contact confirms favorably, the client would be less likely to engage in self-harming behavior.

And example, there are other steps that the psychiatrist can do in advance to help the client not indulge in self-harming behaviour, such as making the client a next day date, educating the client in the use of pain management skills, and providing a lot of support by reminding the client that he knows how challenging this is.

Let's look at an example: Jennifer, a stay-at-home parent, was having trouble working and had started going back to bed in the morning after sending her daughter away to school. She slept until midday, and then became very nervous to get the house cleaned up and dinner made before she got home. To that this fear and make Jennifer feel more successful, after getting her daughter off to school we set a goal for her not to go back to bed. I know Jennifer respects our friendship and sees it improving better as I validate it, so the possibility here is that if I affirm her, she'll be more likely to engage in the conduct that I'm validating in the future again. Therefore, when she comes to our next session and tells me she has achieved this goal three out of five days, I validate her, telling her I recognize how difficult this must have been for her given the extent of the depression she is currently experiencing, and I congratulate her on her partial success. Then we turn to problem solving to see what else we can do in the coming week to increase its success rate.

But if I know Jennifer finds recognition aversive (as some clients do), I'm not going to give validation to the same degree. It's important that I still still support her, because she needs to learn to embrace affirmation in the long run and provide it for herself. But if I overdo it, my approval will become a negative consequence that could effectively prevent her from behaving in the future. So I need to learn if my actions, based on her choice, can affect her conduct and then handle the risk by validating a little or more. In this way, I will increase the likelihood in the future that she will eventually indulge in the desired behaviour.

CHAPTER THREE: DIALECTICAL STANCE AND STRATEGIES

Dialectical Stance

Taking a dialectical approach is the psychological equivalent of taking a physically centric position. Your stance defines possible moves. This is hard to pirouette if you hunker down, wide-legged and stuck. If you're moving all your weight to the ball of one foot, it's hard to push with any force, but it could be the only way to reach an outstretched hand. However, taking a centered stance allows for flexible movement, reach, push, or pirouette. A dialectical approach involves following a set of assumptions that establish a core of internal versatility, to combat the way our brains usually get static or tiptoe around in confrontation. They encourage you to move freely to blend in with the moment. The DBT's dialectical stance is defined by three assumptions:

(1) Reality is whole and interrelated;

(2) Reality is complex and in polarity; and

(3) Change is continual and transactional. Taken together they allow you to move flexibly when faced with ambiguity, contradiction, or conflict,

Reality Is Whole and Interrelated

First, a dialectical view holds that reality's existence is systemic, intertwined, and in connection. We're talking as if parts are somehow separate and independent of the whole, yet we recognize at the same time that's just a way to talk. Because of its related connection with the whole, we can only say something is an item or part. Take a simple example like a game of basketball. They may act as though a given individual player's action is separate, yet the behavior of the person is decided by the whole. The defender tracks the opponent closely to guard against a shot when the teams are playing a man-to-man defence. The relations are apparent; a change in player A results in a change in player B. The teams do so as the ball moves. The action of each player directly connects to that of an enemy. Sometimes a part's relation to the whole is less evident, more like a zone defense where the changing role of one player leads to some transition but not as much as in a man-to-man matchup.

Likewise, as we make this statement of relational interdependence in counseling, we may still act as if therapist and client are separate and independent yet when we look deeply we see that they are linked and are part of a larger whole. From this point of view, separacy and sequential simplified causality are less common, also perceived to be misperception. An example of Zen teaching illustrates that well. A Zen master might have an ordinary sheet of paper and ask, "What's that?"Journal," should we say. Natural fiber and the material used to produce the products. Years of rain and sunshine that fed the trees making the pulp. Light waves arising from distant stars; water molecules coming from distant oceans. The employees who harvested the trees were pulping and producing the paper, wrapping it and taking it to the market. All the ties that led the staff to be able to do those tasks: others who developed and cooked their food; others who used each tool to design and create. We see that the piece of paper very simply comprises the whole world. The paper sheet can be said to be essentially "nonpaper components," a moment of many causal cycles moving together in a single space and time that is called "paper" at that instant. The same could be said of the discrete space and time that we call "therapist" or "person." We see this but lack our sense of interdependence when faced with uncertainty and disagreement. When a client does something that we hate (e.g., sends an offensive phone message, requests support that we can not give), our programmed first reaction is for our mind to focus into a static context of The Other doing something to Me that has to be resolved or stopped. We lose track of the fact that the behavior of the client is as much the joining of many causal strands as the piece of paper is. In fact, all the circumstances necessary to cause that moment to arise have occurred. Our own irritation response, our evaluative labels of "problematic" or "inappropriate" are also the result of multiple conditions coming together. For instance, given different professional training, we may be delighted (rather than irritated) when clients do what happens elsewhere in life with us— we get to work directly on that.

This belief that truth is whole, connected, and in relation, contributes to seeing that all is induced, and thus could not be otherwise in a profound sense. Both client and therapist responses, even when we can not see the causal web, are caused equally. This means that not only the client but also the relationships between the client, the community of the client, the therapist, and the community of the therapist are taken into account from a dialectical perspective, assessment and intervention. For examples, we appear to find pathology in the patient in the West. Instead, assessment is directed to the entire system with dialectical views. For instance, the extreme sensitivity of one client was due at least in part to the extreme invalidation of racism he experienced. The extremely dark skin and large size rendered everyday tasks such as a gauntlet of invalidation standing in a grocery checkout while clients instinctively moved away from him or the clerk accidentally stunned and healed with her first look. The therapist and treatment team, informed by dialectical philosophy, strive to view the person in context, especially turning to search the larger causal web to see what is left out of the case formulation when an impasse occurs (dialectical assessment).

Reality Is Complex and in Polarity

Third, a dialectical view holds that nature is fluid, binary, and oppositional. Also, from our experiences and from clinical work, we intuitively understand it. Suppose a runaway

12-year-old (built like a 15-year-old) is admitted by police into a psychiatric unit. The file reveals that as a child he has had horrific physical abuse, and a slight developmental disability. He seems to have manic symptoms with extreme irritability whilst you interview him. The tox screen shows multiple medications. He is admitted for comment. At this point you think, "Huh, there's this and there's that, and then there's this other piece, wow, it's complicated." But then, in a sexually graphic manner, he's physically threatening the little, beloved social worker; now there's high emotion among the staff. So long as someone on the inpatient unit takes the position of being consistent on the requirements of the procedure, it elicits an explanation of why no exceptions to the law should be made in this situation. Another person thinks the patient can be discharged fairly, which causes somebody else in the team to give arguments that this is not a good idea. In oppositional or divisive ways, we always respond to the challenge. The life of' yes' gives rise to' no;" everything' to' nothing.' Perhaps it is the essence of truth or perhaps just the nature of human thought or expression. Whatever the cause, we sometimes collapse into systems where there is conflict between oppositional components. As applied to human confrontation, all competing views can often be correct or contain elements of the facts (for example, there are valid grounds for discharge and withhold discharge). These first two dialectical premises, taken together, mean that no one ever has a "whole" view on a customer. Therapists are like the blind men who each approach a part of an elephant and who are certain that the whole is just the same as the section that they touch. "An elephant is large and fluffy," "no, no, long, round, and small," "no, no, no, sturdy like a wall." Everyone is real and everyone is incomplete.

Intelligent, rational people will disagree with this opinion, though. When the problems are complex, polarized divergent opinions are seen as inevitable. There's nothing wrong: the client doesn't break the team pathologically; the therapist isn't (necessarily) arrogant or narcissistic. It's just the essence of the phenomena. No one on a treatment team has the facts secured. Any understanding is probably somewhat partial and something important is missing. Thus DBT places great focus on dialogs leading to synthesis. How does the piece I keep match yours to make it a whole that is more complete, cohesive or workable? Together we are searching for what is right in divisive or divergent roles, rather than a common front. Rather than settling a dispute arbitrarily by lowering one end of the dialectic or struggling for only one (my!) position, an effort is made to remain engaged without appeasing, capitulating, dominating or acknowledging the invalid.

Change Is Continual and Transactional

Third, a dialectical view holds that, even though it may be so gradual, it is hard to notice if you look deeply, transition is constant. A seed planted in the field is constantly changing—swelling, germinating, developing into a flower and deteriorating into the nutrients that fuel the next seed. Our predominant experience, despite this continuous change, is of continuity. We perceive the consistency of our physical bodies when all of our bodies' molecules have actually changed. Sometimes these incremental changes coincide in a sudden change. A concrete overpass melts and thaws, with every truck and vehicle moving infinitesimally until it unexpectedly breaks and collapses. The premise here is that nature as a whole is in motion: you can never repeatedly (Heraclitus) walk into the same flow. Most of our minds see unchanging consistency, but continuous transition is more important from a dialectical viewpoint. Dynamic continuity interpretation is an artefact or misperception.

Identity is also viewed as dynamic and constantly changing. The only reason he looks old is that she looks younger; the only reason I look rigid is that you're versatile. If a new, stiffer person joins our team so immediately, by contrast, I seem very agile. Having a dialectical view suggests that words like "good" or "evil" or "dysfunctional" are the person's historical memories, not the person's intrinsic attributes. My main examples come from looking over time at advisory teams or teaching skills classes. Whoever happens to be the most (pick your adjective: negative / positive, task-focused / process-focused) makes the most of us insane. Yet if people are forced to live in the situation, there is always something going on and they adjust, even drastically. Once a client had been "a issue" in a skills training program, delivering constant negative feedback and blunt but whip-smart criticism. The lead ability teacher, by comparison, seemed like a conservative Pollyanna. He shared the same style of sarcastic humor as "the problem client" when anew co-trainer rotated into the skills group, but instead of being harsh he had a delightful, wry smile. He appreciated the lead skills teacher, and enjoyed it. Team dynamics converted critique into humor and built a feedback loop that was lighter but still pointed. The group leader, freed from the siege mentality and now actually seeing the fun in it all, became more imaginative and likable herself. The "client problem" had less to criticize, and was able to learn more easily. Things settled (until the next person on "problem" arose!).

Dialectics in Balancing Goals

Maintaining a dialectical stance can be difficult for therapists, because the pull is to be locked into a concept at either end of the pole instead of experiencing directly how two truths stand side by side as part of a larger synthesis. This can be particularly difficult for two of the main goals of DBT — increasing regulation of client emotion and decreasing priority targets such as self-injury. For this function, the DBT clinicians view these two purposes in dialectical terms.

Dialectics of Emotion Regulation

DBT sets out a dialectical goal for regulation of emotions. Clients are learning skills to change feelings and embrace emotions as they are. Such views seem inconsistent in the abstract, a mixed message about how to respond to private experience. Yet if we look at our actual experience, the problem will overcome. The most difficult moments of our lives often require our emotional responses to be both regulated (changed) and consciously experienced (accepted).

Consider a clinical example here. A client, lost primary custody of her 2-year-old daughter in bitter divorce proceedings. The husband's counsel has built up a misleading history of her past psychiatric hospitalizations and attempted suicide, successfully denying her most recent progress in therapy. Anyone would be anxious to lose custody, particularly when one's own transgressions contributed to the decision. Her emotions were however at an unrelenting, all-consuming intensity for this client. She was mad about suffering. Connection with her ex-husband has been like a flame to fire, both in real life and in fantasy. Her agony will kindle in hallucinations of anger and vengeance. She loathed herself, sure that his claim that she was a terrible mother was true and that without her, her daughter would be better off. Every time she imagined a future without living day to day with her daughter, she sobbed, grief-stricken. Instead of enduring the pain, she had urges to capitulate and give up visitation. She sat in shock, detached and numb for hours But she had little time to sort out these feelings to inform her next set of actions because the court required her to begin mediation in order to determine the privileges of visitation. The firm needed to demonstrate the integrity to build legitimacy and better negotiate terms for the consultation. The head was in an upheaval in these emotionally challenging encounters with the court or its ex-husband. Yet if she even displayed a whiff of dysregulation of the emotions, her husband would use it against her. In the case her aims required excellent control of emotions.

Based on the study of the chain, the therapist and client defined shame as the primary emotion which contributed to the most escape through problem-solving responses. This was especially the case when the client heard or felt she was "a bad mother." During one extended session, the client and psychiatrist unflinchingly looked at how this accusation became true: that is, the client described all the reasons she had disappointed her daughter and failed to meet her own standards. When mentioned in the last segment, the psychiatrist used affirmation to keep the client in episodes of casual communication so she could feel guilt without fleeing into inappropriate secondary responses. Validation always took care of resilient emotions: the explanation for her pain and guilt was how much she loved her daughter and wanted the best, how badly she longed to be a good mother.

The client and therapist exercised the revolutionary recognition DBT technique, looking at the causal network that produced all the conditions that led to the deficiencies as a person, without sugarcoating the harm done by the child. Also instinctively and with the aid of the therapist, the client learned how the guilt turned into deep regret and the positive intervention recommended that the harm be remedied and restored. She found a kernel of pride at how fiercely her daughter used this therapy to change in order to do better. The woman even fought with her husband with anger. Here the therapist actively helped the client regulate anger and avoid signs of anger to avoid physically or verbally attacking her husband or property (which she had done many times in the past). The client's friends, for example, loyally sided with her and fuelled her anger by doing things like using the husband's picture as a dartboard, plotting to ruin his reputation at work, and endlessly talking about how unfair he was. The client asked her friends to change tactics with her in the lead up to the counseling meeting: either they spoke about the situations in a totally low-key non-judgmental way (e.g., "divorces are really rough," "there are things about this case that I don't like") or they ignored the subject and focused on ways where the client was building a new life.

In addition, the client and therapist identified the two most anger-causing things the husband did and practiced drills where the therapist presented the indications and the client deliberately changed her breathing to calm down. At the end of the exhalation she inhaled for a count of 3, held her breath for a count of 2, then exhaled for 5, slowly and fully, pausing for 2 counts. She actively imagined in this practice picking up every thought or emotion about her situation and putting it in a box, saying "later" gently. She practiced this exercise and radical acceptance of shame on her own while looking at a picture of her husband holding their daughter. She put the picture in a box repeatedly and then pulled it out to look at the picture and exercise again. The client learned how to monitor her attention to make interaction with emotional messages more accurate. She also learned to withdraw from signs of emotion so as to down-regulate anger. From a dialectical perspective, both approaches are valid, and the focus has been on helping the client discriminate when either strategy has or has not at the moment fit their goals.

Dialectical Abstinence

Another traditional DBT target, dialectical abstinence, contains two seemingly contradictory aspects of one vision. The psychiatrist advises the client to agree immediately and permanently, without exception, to curb the problem behavior (e.g., using drugs or deliberate self-injury). The therapist adopts, one moment at a time, a constant insistence on total abstinence. The message conveyed is that it would be disastrous to engage in the problem behavior again. At the same time, if a lapse occurs, the therapist takes a problem-solving, non-judgmental approach to prevention of relapse. In Marlatt's (Marlatt and Donovan, 2005) prolapse technique, the goal is to mitigate "the impact of abstinence failure." After a break, we frequently feel intense depressive emotions and thoughts (e.g., "What's the point? I've already lost it. I could just as well go for it."). The psychiatrist who employs a dialectical technique, when there is a delay, lets the client recognize factors that led to the failure in order to formulate a plan to prevent those lapses in future. The psychiatrist then applies for a recommendation of total abstinence. Through contrast, dialectical abstinence, when caught in a snowstorm, is like hiking an ice path to safety. If you don't keep climbing you could die. Any slip is potentially life threatening. Hence 100 percent of your energy is used to stay on your feet and move. Even if you're down, you're up. You get back straight to putting 100 percent of your energy into moving forward and not falling. If you're a surgeon, nicking arteries are the same. You pay 100% attention to the technique that is flawless; and if you make a mistake, you easily patch it. Then the job is returned to 100 per cent of focus.

Devil's Advocate

Playing the advocate of the devil is a technique used in the early stages of therapy in an attempt to obtain customer commitment to engage in DBT, but it is also a useful strategy at other therapy points. The purpose of this approach is that the therapist can help the client advocate for it by reasoning against something, and a resolution can be reached through that process. Returning to my client who was dealing with binge eating, let's take a look at how I used this technique to help affirm her commitment to change: therapist: you tell me you want to avoid bingeing, but at the same time you remind me that you just want to snack when you have the desire you don't want to use ability. Do you really think you are committed to stopping the bingeing?

Customer: Absolutely. I am engaged. I know I just got ta stop.

Therapist: Knowing that you need to stop and wanting to stop are two things. Did you feel genuinely dedicated to this objective?

Client: Indeed it does. I just want to focus on it. I am gaining so much weight and I have high cholesterol. I know that gives me trouble with the fitness.

Therapist: Maybe, but you have known that your cholesterol is high and your weight gets out of control for quite some time now. What's new now that suddenly makes you want to stop? Or what do you think you can do to help you stop?

Client: I just wanted to make a rest. I really didn't see a way to do it, because it's so complicated. I remember we talked about a lot of things, and perhaps I just didn't put as much effort as I could into it. I think I need to go back and review the skills we've already talked about, which will help me stop; for example, when the urge comes up, be mindful and choose to distract myself from the urge rather than just act on it.

Therapist: All right, this sounds like a great place to get going.

From this example, you can see that the therapist did not tell the client that she thought she wasn't committed, or that I thought she couldn't stop bingeing. The aim is not to be dismissive, but to challenge or disagree with clients in a way that makes them care about the other side and fight for it. Sometimes it helps them, as in this instance, to generate a solution that they will be more likely to implement, since it was their idea.

Use of Metaphor

Linehan (1993a) states that using metaphors is an effective, insightful way to teach clients how to think dialectically, and to open up the possibility of behaving in a new way. The use of metaphors in therapy is of course not unique to DBT; it has been stressed in many psychotherapies and is also often used informally in therapy. One should not underestimate its effectiveness. Lankton and Lankton (1989) note that psychological metaphors do not elicit the same kind of reaction to new ideas that may often be driving suggestions; instead, they are viewed as a more gentle way to accept improvements.

The use of metaphors in therapy may be helpful in many ways, including the following, according to Lyddon, Clay, and Sparks (2001):

- Establishing relationships with clients

- Assisting clients in accessing their emotions

- Challenging client beliefs

- Working with client resistance (in DBT terms, helping therapists and clients get rid of dialectical dilemmas)

Linehan (1993a) points out some additional factors that make metaphors relevant in counseling, including the fact that stories are more compelling and therefore easier to remember; that metaphors are versatile, allowing clients to use them for various reasons and in their own way, which also gives them a sense of autonomy; and that stories can be less intrusive, as is the point of the story I The main purpose of using metaphors as a dialectical technique is for the therapist to express acceptance and understanding of where the clients are at present and, at the same time, to present an alternative that will help clients progress towards improvement. When the psychiatrist explains the client's emotional dysregulation as the equivalent of having third-degree burns all over her body, the client also feels that the therapist understands the pain she is in and recognizes the need to do something to ensure the burns recover. Here's a short conversation with another case of metaphor usage:

Client: I'm just not sure how much longer I can deal with all that's going on. I sound like I'm stuck on a cliff's edge and I'm not that confident I don't want to fall.

Therapist: Jumping is not the only option. You could also take the climbing equipment that I hold, and climb down that cliff slowly. That's what DBT competencies are for.

Wickman, Daniels, White and Fesmire (1999) find out that when they use the client's own vocabulary, the comparison will be more powerful. In other terms, go with the metaphors the customer provides wherever possible, as in the above case, since the customer naturally relates with them.

Making Lemonade Out of Lemons

You have heard the saying "make lemonade from lemons" or some variant thereof. It allows clinicians in DBT to take an obvious problem and turn it into something positive. As Linehan (1993a) points out, this is another skill that needs to be used with caution so that it doesn't seem like invalidating the client or minimizing the problem's seriousness. To use her metaphor, "The therapist's strength is to see the silver lining by admitting that the cloud is actually black" Here's an example: Client: I'm just having a hard time coming to group because I can't stand Michael. He is always talking and never gives anybody else an opportunity to speak in group. He drives me nuts.

Therapist: This is great news, as we've been looking for opportunities for you to treatment non-judgmental practice!

The therapist would then discuss ways she could exercise non-judgmental in collaboration with the client, as well as other related skills where appropriate.

CHAPTER FOUR: PREPARING FOR THE INDIVIDUAL SESSION; WHAT YOU NEED TO KNOW

Over the years, many studies have shown that a positive therapist-client relationship has more effect on outcome than the actual treatment modality itself (e.g., Bordin, 1979; Martin, Garske, & Davis, 2000). Given the range of challenges experienced by people with emotional dysregulation and the way their dysfunctional environments contribute to interactions that are often stressful, clinicians often have an aversion to interacting with such clients. Luckily, DBT helps therapists change their preconceived conceptions about these clients and helps them develop the all-important therapeutic alliance.

DBT ASSUMPTIONS

The following sections are based on the assumptions set forth by Linehan (1993a):

Clients Are Doing Their Best

In counseling, clients (especially those who have trouble controlling their emotions) are often viewed as either not trying hard enough or even engaging in negative or self-destructive activities as a way of getting attention or satisfying some need. The belief that people do their best reminds the psychiatrist that the client is usually coping as well as she can with what she has and what she learns, despite her condition. This assumption reminds the therapist that not everyone grows up learning what they need to know about managing their emotions and problem solving. If you can keep this hypothesis in mind, it will enhance your ability to empathize with clients and teach them the skills they need to do better, rather than blaming them for their life problems.

Clients Want to Get Better

There is a belief in Buddhism that one of the human beings ' motives is to reduce their pain. I think it's safe to say that if clients come for counseling, they want to see some positive life changes. If you're working in a setting where you see mandated clients, this may not, of course, be true; but even then, you're likely to find something the client would really like to change — such as not being involved in criminal justice. Nonetheless, if you go to a group that assumes the opposite — that the individual doesn't want to improve— how inspired do you think you're going to help? Remembering this hypothesis— that clients want to experience less suffering and more happiness in their lives— will help you reduce your judgments and help you more.

Clients Need to Work Harder and Be More Motivated to Make Changes in Their Lives

One of DBT's dialectical dilemmas is the recognition that clients are doing their best with the resources they have and, at the same time, we need to teach them skills that will help them try harder, be more effective and be more motivated to change their lives. In this way, placing responsibility on clients (with the therapist right next to them, teaching and coaching them to use skills), helps keep the therapist motivated to work with clients, as it reminds us that we are not here to "fix" clients, but to help them create a life worth living with (Linehan, 1993a).

Even if clients have not created their problems, they still have to solve them

Understanding that clients must be their own agents of change, rather than relying on others to make changes for them, takes a lot of pressure off therapists by reminding us (and clients) that we can't fix them. Alternatively, people need to solve their own problems, with the educator as the mentor or instructor to help them learn the tools they need to do so. This is the case even though a client wasn't the cause of the problems that she currently faces. The invalidating environment is a perfect example of this: when growing up, the client may have experienced omnipresent invalidation which, in combination with emotional vulnerability, has led to their emotional regulation problems. While it is clearly not the fault of the customer that she is having such issues, if she doesn't try to fix her problems, nothing will improve and she will continue to suffer. Having this idea in mind will also help to reduce the burnout of therapists by educating you that your job as a therapist is to educate people how to solve the problem they have never experienced as children.

The Lives of Suicidal Clients Is Unbearable

They will take the pain that clients convey to us at face value. Instead of trying to figure out what their ulterior motives is, when a victim commits suicide, you will presume that she tried to kill herself because she considered her life unbearably unbearable! This presumption also helps remind you that the customer is highly sensitive to feelings. You may have heard the comparison in which the BPD person is contrasted with an adult who has had third-degree burns (Linehan, 1993a). How can life bearable with this kind of emotional pain for someone wandering around and no experience to help manage it? This presumption lets you create or maintain a positive working relationship with such clients because you affirm your ability to empathize with them, rather than blame them for their actions.

Clients Need to Learn How to Act Skillfully in All Areas of Their Lives

Many of us have met clients who struggle to regulate their emotions but have succeeded in their professions as teachers, lawyers, executives and so on. What's easy to forget is that just because these clients can use skills in one area of life doesn't mean that they can transfer these skills to another. When you forget that, you are likely to give the same invalidating message to clients that they have gotten for years: that they should be able to solve the problem. The second part of the premise clients need to learn how to act skillfully is that this learning will come in different situations when they are learning new skills, including stressful situations where their feelings are strong. This is one reason why it is best not to hospitalize clients in the DBT model: the development desired can only happen if clients live in their setting

Clients Cannot Fail in Psychotherapy

They do not blame people with cancer if chemo doesn't succeed. If someone hurts her ankle, and after six weeks in a cast, it doesn't recover, we don't tell her she's disappointed. So why would we fault the client for not getting psychotherapy working? If a client is not progressing or dropping out of therapy, it is not the fault of the client; rather, the fault lies with the therapy, the therapist or both. In other words, either the therapy mode is simply not right for the client or the therapist has not been effective in implementing the treatment with the client. This can also help when considering any past treatments that have not worked for the client. Remembering that it wasn't the client who failed the counseling but the therapist that failed the client will make you motivated to work with the client and find something to improve. Rest assured, though, that if the client doesn't get better or drops out of treatment the focus is not on blaming the psychiatrist. Obviously as clinicians we want to make sure we do our best to implement the procedure, so use that theory as a way to motivate yourself to do the part. If a client shows no improvement and you know that the client is unable to fail in therapy, you will examine your skills and see how effective you are in implementing therapy, rather than simply attributing lack of progress to the "resistance" of the client.

Therapists Treating Clients with Emotion Dysregulation Need Support Themselves

BPD and dysregulation of the mind in general are among the most difficult psychotherapy disorders to deal with. Because of these clients' high emotional vulnerability, it is common for therapists to unintentionally invalidate or otherwise alienate them, so that treatment stops, sometimes quite suddenly. Even when there is a good collaborative relationship, non-DBT therapists often do not participate in giving certain clients the skills they require or do not balance the professional learned with approval. These are just a few of the reasons that therapists who handle these clients deserve help, and why DBT puts such emphasis on the treatment team, too. The team may be a consultant or supervisor, or it may be a full DBT treatment team, says Linehan (1993a). Whatever the format, the therapist's idea is therapy to increase the likelihood of success in treating clients with emotional dysregulation.

REDUCING THERAPIST BURNOUT WITH DBT

Keeping in mind the DBT assumptions about clients helps us as therapists to bring empathy and compassion to our clients, rather than falling into the judgments that often take hold when working with BPD clients or emotional dysregulation problems. The ability to understand and empathize with these high-needed clients instead of judging or blaming them helps prevent therapist burnout in addition to facilitating therapy. Two other DBT elements also play a role in avoiding burnout: our shortcomings are identified and what Linehan terms "patient assessment"

Observing Limits

Most of the therapists were taught to set client boundaries. This emphasis on setting proper boundaries, particularly with BPD clients, reflects the commonly held belief that the disease prevents them from being able to act "appropriately" (or, even worse, makes them want to act "inappropriately") and leads clients to cross the boundaries of other people, including the therapist. In DBT, neither the client nor the therapist is seen as disordered; in other words, if a client calls her therapist every day, she isn't too needy and doesn't try to manipulate. Likewise, the psychiatrist is not too forgiving for receiving phone calls from the client, nor is the therapist having problems with countertransference. Rather than pathologize the client or the therapist for having poor limits, the presumption of DBT is that there is clearly a difference, or poor fit, between what one person wants and what the other is willing or capable of offering. There are, of course, certain hard-and-fast lines that we do not reach as therapists: intimate relationships with clients or other situations in which clients might be abused in some way. (See the rules of the regulating body of your discipline, if you're not sure what I'm referring to.) But other than that, it's important to realize that the boundaries of everyone are different and vary depending on a variety of factors. Such considerations for therapy include your interaction with the client, other stressors in your life at a given time, the autonomy you've provided your career and the environment in which you're working, etc. Let's look at an example: In my work, receiving text messages, texts, or phone calls from clients outside of the session is quite common for me. Generally speaking, I think that people don't use this opportunity very often or for no good reason— for example, when they need ability counseling when they feel very nervous, have suicidal thoughts, or decide not to act on an undesirable impulse. But I have other limits: all my clients know that when I go to bed, I turn off my cell phone, so I'm not available in the hours of the overnight. I'm not going to take phone calls or check through texts or emails while I'm with other clients so I may not be able to answer instantly. But there are some more individual limitations. With one person with whom I have worked for about two years, I have a cap that she is not going to approach me about a question until she has used some skills to try to support her. For someone I've just started working with, I wouldn't have this cap, since that person wouldn't have mastered the necessary skills yet. On the other end of the spectrum, I have a friend that I just began to see who was having trouble doing assignments outside of training. Every other day I give the customer a text message to ask her to do her homework. I wouldn't do this to the person I've been dealing with for two years, because at this stage of counseling, she doesn't need that kind of help.

Our limitations as therapists should evidently vary to reflect the client and the context. Although you don't want to be rigid and inconsistent, understanding that boundaries shouldn't be set and unchangeable is essential. You may be able to do something for a week that you will not do next week. They may be able to do something another psychiatrist does not want to do and vice versa. That doesn't make it right or wrong, or right or wrong; it's just a fact of life that everyone has different limits.

SETTING BOUNDARIES VS. OBSERVING LIMITS

When you think of the word "reaching limits" as opposed to "observing boundaries," it would seem far less flexible. A fence is more precise and immovable than a border. Therefore, once you create a threshold, then it becomes the duty of the company not to cross the boundary, and any action that exceeds the boundary is pathologized and deemed inappropriate. On the other hand, if you follow your limitations, it is your responsibility to keep your limits when the actions of the client that surpasses them. It means that it's not about the inappropriateness of the actions of the customer but about your own personal and professional interests. Observing our boundaries also requires better consumer contact. Keeping in mind that the borders of everyone are special and changeable (as opposed to a border that is more of an immovable barrier), whether in counseling or in daily life, how can we trust our clients to recognize our limits on earth?

As with anything, the first step in knowing the boundaries is to become mindful of them. This means monitoring your burnout level with clients, and checking your willingness in sessions. Reflect on your boundaries if you're criticizing or accusing the client: Is there anything you need to change? If so, it is important to be honest about this with the client. If you don't convey that cap, you're going to burn out, reducing the likelihood that consumer counseling will actually advance. While it may be difficult to express a limit to the client, remember that it will reduce your burnout feelings and make you more effective in the long-term therapeutic relationship.

Don't mistake this to mean observing your limits is for the benefit of the customer. It's for the good of you. Observing your limits is your duty, not the customer's, so be sure to make that about you While, of course, you need to stick to your limits and disclose them to clients, occasionally extending your limits is also necessary. Of example, if you don't usually take phone calls on weekends but you've got a customer who's dealing with a difficult situation and need some extra coaching skills, you could tell her she can contact you on a particular weekend. In reaction to behavioral aggression, however, don't stretch your boundaries.

You just need to be mindful that extending the boundaries when, for example, a customer threatens suicide is not beneficial and simply will make it more likely that this will happen again in the future. Alternatively, if a behaviour escalates, keep maintaining the boundaries while also validating the frustration of the client and helping her find other ways to deal with the issue.

WHAT TO DO WITH YOUR LIMITS

First and foremost, explaining your boundaries to your clients is crucial. That is not to say that in the first session, you should give each client a list of your limits. As one thing, it's impossible to predict when conditions with a particular client will occur that will force you to set limits. There may be some limitations that need to be expressed immediately. For example, it is common practice that there will be a fee if a client does not show up for an appointment and does not give you twenty-four hours ' notice; that is a limit. Here are just a few more common examples. Think about your limitations in these areas:

• Frequency and number of sessions: Do you see clients once per week? Each two weeks? How often would they like to be seen? Have you had a limited number of sessions, or can a customer be used for ever? Besides being a question of your preferences, these can also depend on the policies of your employer.

• Length of sessions: How long are the sessions? Are you flexible in doing so? For example, if a client is in a crisis, do you want to extend the session length? Once again, this may depend on your place of work.

• Calls by phone: Can you take customer phone calls in sessions? If so, how frequently? Do you have a phone-call time frame? Do you accept calls, for example, only during business hours, or at other times?

These are just a few examples and the question will arise in an infinite number of ways as to what your limits are. The aim is to express the shortcomings as these situations arise to clients. Let yourself be versatile, and allow yourself to change. If you think about circumstances in your everyday personal life, it can help: If a friend is twenty minutes late for dinner and doesn't contact you, is that good, or do you let her know you'd like a phone call? That is a cap if you want a phone call. If a friend is calling you in the middle of the night, are you going to answer the phone? If not, for you, that's a cap. You may have a tradition that you stay at home with your wife for one weekend of the month just to spend time together and nothing can mess with that couple of times. That's a limit. Of course, you may not typically like a phone call in the middle of the night, but you bend that rule when you find out that a friend's mother just died. You may not usually allow anything to interfere with your couple time but you are more flexible on a weekend when your best friend moves and needs some help. These kinds of things also occur in therapy.

Consultation to the Client

While knowing the weaknesses, the DBT idea of patient feedback will help minimize burnout and increase treatment efficacy. Consultation with the client essentially means the function of the individual therapist is to advise the client how to communicate with others, rather than advising others how they should interact with the client or speak on behalf of the client. In other words, people should consult with the customer about their needs, rather than consult you. This could include anyone in the life of the client: families, colleagues, other health-care professionals, etc. Let's look at an example to make this theory clearer: Julie is a twenty-seven-year-old woman with trouble controlling her feelings, who recently started attending a training group on DBT skills at her local hospital. She's been seeing her individual therapist for about six months, and they both decided that she would find the DBT skills helpful. After her second week of group, however, Julie told her individual therapist she was considering dropping out of the group because she found it too hard. For clarification of this, a non-DBT practitioner may contact the community facilitator. However, in consultation with the client, the DBT therapist would instead discuss the issue with the client and coach her on the use of skills so she could speak to the group facilitator herself.

This sometimes plays out a bit differently: It is expected that the individual DBT therapist will tell other professionals how to deal with the client. Sometimes this expectation is the client; the therapist, for example, wants to contact the local emergency department to advocate that she be admitted because she feels suicidal. Instead of doing so, the DBT therapist would be coaching the client to use skills to meet their needs. Other times the expectation is that of another professional; for example, a local emergency department nurse calling to say the client will not be admitted and asking what to do with her. As Linehan (1993a) says, the driving guideline here is for the practitioners to follow their normal procedures. In other words, note that the environment will not necessarily change just because the consumer has trouble controlling their emotions; thus, it is up to the customer to learn how to handle this skillfully.

Most people often run into this problem when working with teens whose parents try to help them with their problems more effectively. Quite often a parent will ask me to meet without the teen present, in which case I'll answer that this is not part of my practice. The client present must say anything they wish to say. If a parent contacts me through a phone call, I'll explain that the call's content will be communicated to the client. Of example, when relating to family members or friends of clients, it is vital to be validating and empathetic, but it is of utmost importance to consider who your client is, and that she needs to learn how to express herself and deal with these kinds of experiences on her own, with you providing training tools to help her to do so.

Therefore, working with the company is about helping clients develop the problem-solving skills they have never mastered as children so that they can rely less on others and more on themselves slowly. This makes them take responsibility for their own lives, rather than acting on behalf of others.

STAGES OF TREATMENT

A sequence of steps through which clients advance towards recovery: pretreatment, acquisition of essential abilities (stage 1), elimination of post-traumatic stress (stage 2), and increased self-respect and accomplishment of goals (stage 3). I'll describe each of Linehan's phases in the remainder of this essay. Throughout the remainder of this book, though, the emphasis is on step 1 therapy, as this is the cornerstone of the DBT paradigm as it is today. Therapeutic at other levels of intervention would use a mixture of other therapeutic methods; in stage 2, for example, the psychiatrist would use PTSD-specific treatment models, such as CBT or sensorimotor therapy.

Pretreatment Stage: Orientation and Commitment

Sadly, in people with emotional dysregulation, premature cessation of treatment is by no means rare. Linehan (1993a) discusses a study by Parloff, Waskow, and Wolfe (1978) that illustrated a correlation between the use of techniques for pretreatment orientation and a decrease in dropout rates for therapy. Since the dropout rate for these individuals continues to be high, the first several individual DBT meetings focus on having the client and the psychiatrist determine whether they are willing and capable of working together. The psychiatrist also encourages the person in these early stages to change certain assumptions or expectations about counseling that could lead to negative consequences of care, such as premature termination (Linehan, 1993a). The psychiatrist also focuses on conducting an assessment with the client, delivering psychoeducation on the condition of the client, and ensuring a contribution to both general treatment and specific goals.

Stage 1: Attaining Basic Capacities

Once the psychiatrist and counselor have dedicated themselves to working together, treatment reaches step 1, focusing on habits that pose a direct threat to the safety and stability of the person (Swales & Heard, 2009). At this point, the goal is to reduce suicidal actions and emotions, as well as other activities that are destabilizing, self-destructive, or otherwise harmful, and resolve ability deficits. A lot of time in conventional CBT would be spent moving from one problem to another, making it difficult for the practitioner to find time to teach the strategies that the person needs to manage feelings. To address these issues in a productive manner, DBT organizes the daily session in a methodical way that provides emotional dysregulation with much required consistency for clients. The customer's Behavior Monitoring Sheet includes this framework, which is a short form of journaling. There are various types of monitoring pads, and you can tailor them for different clients. I also included in this section a replica of the one I use later; please feel free to photocopy it and use it in your case. From this recording pad, the following sequence discusses habits

1. Behaviors that interfere with life

2. Behaviors that interfere with therapy

3. Behaviors that interfere with quality of life

Note that with highly dysfunctional and depressed people, eliminating habits that conflict with life or interfere with therapy can require longer than one year of treatment. He says, however, that by the completion of the first year of treatment, "patients should also have at least a working knowledge and skill in the main coping skills taught in DBT." Keep in mind that having a working knowledge of the techniques does not guarantee that clients will apply it to all their issues!

BEHAVIORS THAT INTERFERE WITH LIFE

The first topics to be discussed in individual sessions are life-interfering habits, in the following order:

1. Any suicidal behaviors

2. Nonsuicidal self-harming behaviors, such as cutting or burning

3. Intrusive suicidal or homicidal urges or communications

4. Suicidal ideation

When these kinds of actions emerge outside the group, in the next person session they become a topic for conversation. Through DBT, behavior analysis (BA) is the technique most widely used to tackle certain types of behaviours. The BA lets psychiatrist and counselor take a thorough look at the factors that contribute to a desired behaviour and encourage the client to continue to engage in the action of the problem.

Remember that suicidal thoughts that are present as background noise frequently or continuously are not always addressed directly in the therapy session, as this could discourage therapist and counselor from focusing on other problem behaviors. The DBT theory is that this form of suicidal thinking has to do with the low quality of life arising from emotional dysregulation, so the emphasis on improving quality of life (which is the third goal on the agenda) should address this issue.

BEHAVIORS THAT INTERFERE WITH THERAPY

The second subject to be discussed is activities that in some way conflict specifically with the client's treatment, from the most damaging to the least harmful. Such habits may appear in many different ways, and may include both client and therapist. Symptoms include the client or psychiatrist who is late or cancels meetings, who is not properly prepared for treatments (e.g., the client has not finished her monitoring sheet or the therapist has not read her notes to remind herself what assignment was assigned), taking phone calls between sessions, etc. Such habits can also be more nuanced, such as the therapist pressuring the client too far, invalidating the client, or reinforcing the client's unhealthy behaviors, or either the client or the therapist avoiding discussing difficult session subjects. Behaviors that conflict with treatment can also become more harmful (for example, the therapist does not follow a danger cap with the client or the counselor, or the psychiatrist, in some way).

BEHAVIORS THAT INTERFERE WITH QUALITY OF LIFE

The final item on the agenda for each session addresses behaviors that interfere with the quality of life of the client. This could include symptoms of comorbid depression, anxiety, or substance abuse; inadequate accommodation or financial hardship; or lack of social care. Since clients with emotional dysregulation typically have many of these external problems in their lives, it's important to decide which area to focus on is most important. Second, fix immediate problems such as accommodation or completing a rehabilitation program; second, resolve more solvable problems and approach the more difficult things later; and third, target activities linked to the two higher-order priorities (behaviors that conflict with life and those that interfere with therapy).

PUTTING IT ALL TOGETHER

Please recap the three previous parts to make the expectations of the care targets clear, here is

1. Suicidal behaviors and nonsuicidal self-harming behaviors

2. Behaviors that interfere with therapy

3. Suicidal ideation and "misery"

4. Maintaining treatment gains

5. Other goals the client identifies

Stage 2: Reducing Post-traumatic Stress

DBT does not focus on the symptoms of PTSD until clients have the skills required. When clients engage in or experience urges to engage in suicide, self-harm, substance use, and other self-destructive behaviors on a regular basis, not only are they unprepared, it is actually unsafe to do this kind of work. This does not mean that the trauma history of the client during stage 1 is ignored. If the client brings these issues up in therapy, the practitioner validates the pain and suffering felt by the client, but the focus remains on the present — how the stress is likely to contribute to problem behaviors, and the strategies that the person can use to help reduce these activities.

In this stage 2, The trauma becomes the focus, and the exposure therapy is used to process past traumas emotionally. Swales and Heard (2009) note that since not all people have a trauma background, stage 2 may also concentrate on negative relationship interactions due to emotional dysregulation and resulting loss of interpersonal skills for the client. While these experiences may not be destabilizing, they can still, if left unresolved, contribute to ongoing pain and problem behaviours.

Stage 3: Increasing Self-Respect and Achieving Individual Goals

In stage 3, the aim becomes to help clients begin to trust, value and respect themselves, as well as to continue working and generalize the lessons they have gained in counseling to the rest of their lives. Linehan (1993a) points out that switching between stages in a nonlinear fashion is not uncommon for clients; for example, going from stage 1 to stage 2, back to stage 1, then shifting to stage 3 etc. She also stresses the importance of taking breaks when necessary; for example, before going from the relative stability of completing stage 1 work to starting the work on stage 2.

CPSIA information can be obtained
at www.ICGtesting.com
Printed in the USA
LVHW080454090322
712998LV00004B/120